THE SCIENCE
OF BEING GREAT

THE SCIENCE
OF BEING GREAT

by Wallace D. Wattles

The Secret to Living Your Greatest Life Now
From the Author of
The Science of Getting Rich

Abridged and Introduced
by Mitch Horowitz

THE CONDENSED ██ CLASSICS LIBRARY™

MEDIA

Published by Gildan Media LLC
aka G&D Media.
www.GandDmedia.com

The Science of Being Great was originally published in 1911
G&D Media Condensed Classics edition published 2018
Abridgement and Introduction copyright © 2017 by Mitch
Horowitz

FIRST EDITION: 2018

Cover design by David Rheinhardt of Pyrographx

Interior design by Meghan Day Healey of Story Horse, LLC.

ISBN: 978-1-7225-0047-4

Contents

"You Can Become What You Want to Be"

The title of this preface is the final line of author Wallace D. Wattles's opening chapter, and the heart of this book. But it is more than an author's credo. It is, in a sense, an encapsulation of American metaphysical ideals—the outlook of a still-young nation when Wattles wrote *The Science of Being Great* in 1911, and an outlook still held today.

In the era in which Wattles lived, America was suffused with the influence of a new metaphysics—Christian Science, New Thought, mental healing, and other spiritual philosophies taught modern people to believe that what we think and feel concretizes in the experience of our lives; that thoughts are causative. This spiritual vision harmonized with the sense of limitless possibility that many Americans felt in the early twentieth century, when the nation's growth and expansion seemed endless.

This book, which appeared the year that Wattles died, was, in my view, his greatest work. It captured everything that he saw around him, and put a sharper focus on the ideas that he explored in his widely read book *The Science of Getting Rich*, which preceded this one in 1910.

Wattles was far more than a cheerleader for personal and national growth. He was also a fiery social reformer who was forced out of his Methodist pulpit in northern Indiana after refusing to accept collection-basket offerings from parishioners who ran sweatshops. He believed in a voluntary, democratic socialism, and he foresaw a new world where cooperation would replace animal competition. He ran for office twice on the ticket of Eugene V. Debs's Socialist Party. He advocated for the rights of striking workers and suffragists. Yet his reputation was sealed, and he received posthumous fame in our own time, for a book dedicated to personal money-getting, *The Science of Getting Rich*.

None of this was contradictory. Wattles believed, without any sense of personal conflict, that the potential of the individual must be expressed both socially and materially. "Man is formed for growth," he wrote, "and he is under the necessity of growing. It is essential to his happiness that he should continually advance. Life without progress is unendurable."

Although Wattles had no way of knowing that his life would be lost to tuberculosis at age fifty, shortly after finishing this book, *The Science of Being Great* formed a culminating manifesto and testament to all that he believed. In its pages, abridged to their essential points in this Condensed Classics edition, you will discover Wattles's complete philosophy of life: namely, that each of us is run through by a Divine influx, which can raise us to extraordinary heights of personal excellence, acts of creativity, and skills marked by virtuosity. But to fully place ourselves within this eternal, creative current we must first be in alignment with Gospel ethics, and possess a sense of duty to God and our fellow beings.

Self-refinement, he wrote, is the key to transforming ourselves into vehicles for the Higher Principle of life, or God, which yearns for expression through us, and can deliver us to greatness.

Everything that this good and thoughtful man believed necessary for a powerful life can be found in this short and compelling book. May it deliver you to your greatest heights of achievement—and your deepest sense of responsibility.

—Mitch Horowitz

Chapter One

Any Person May Become Great

There is a Principle of Power in every person. By the intelligent use and direction of this principle, man can develop his own mental faculties. Man has an inherent power by which he may grow in whatsoever direction he pleases.

The possibility is in the Original Substance from which man is made. Genius is Omniscience flowing into man. Genius is more than talent. Talent may merely be one faculty developed out of proportion to other faculties, but genius is the union of man and God in the acts of the soul. Great men are always greater than their deeds. They are in connection with a reserve power that is without limit.

The purpose of life for man is growth, just as the purpose of life for trees and plants is growth. Trees and plants grow automatically and along fixed lines; man can grow as he will. Trees and plants can only develop certain possibilities and characteristics; man can develop any power that is or has been shown by any person, anywhere. Nothing that is possible in spirit is impossible in flesh and blood. Nothing that man can think is impossible in action. Nothing that man can imagine is impossible of realization.

Man is formed for growth, and he is under the necessity of growing.

It is essential to his happiness that he should continuously advance.

Life without progress becomes unendurable. The greater and more harmonious and well-rounded his growth, the happier man will be.

Every man comes into the world with a predisposition to grow along certain lines, and growth is easier for him along those lines than in any other way.

The Principle of Power gives us just what we ask of it; if we only undertake little things, it only gives us power for little things; but if we try to do great things in a great way it gives us all the power there is.

No greater good can come to any man or woman than to become self-active. All the experiences of life are designed by Providence to force men and women into self-activity; to compel them to cease being creatures of circumstances and master their environment.

Nothing was ever in any man that is not in you; no man ever had more spiritual or mental power than you can attain, or did greater things than you can accomplish. You can become what you want to be.

Chapter Two

The Source of Power

Wisdom is the power to perceive the best ends to aim at and the best means for reaching those ends. It is the power to perceive the right thing to do. The man who is wise enough to know the right thing to do, who is good enough to wish to do only the right thing, and who is able and strong enough to do the right thing is a truly great man.

Wisdom is dependent upon knowledge. Man's knowledge is comparatively limited and so his wisdom is small, unless he can connect his mind with a knowledge greater than his own and draw from it, by inspiration, the wisdom that his own limitations deny him. This he can do; this is what the really great men and women have done.

I proceed to give an illustration: Abraham Lincoln had limited education; but he had the power to perceive truth. When Lincoln became president he was surrounded by a multitude of so-called able advisers, hardly any two of whom were agreed. At times they were all opposed to his policies; at times the whole North was opposed to what he proposed to do. But he saw the truth when others were misled by appearances; his judgment was seldom or never wrong. He was at once the ablest statesman and the best solider of the period. Where did he, a comparatively unlearned man, get this wisdom?

Knowledge of truth is not often reached by the processes of reason. It was due to spiritual insight. He perceived truth. But where did he perceive it and whence did the perception come? We see something similar in Washington, whose faith and courage, due to his perception of truth, held the colonies together during the long and often apparently hopeless struggle of the Revolution.

We discover back of Washington and Lincoln something greater than either Washington or Lincoln. We see the same thing in all great men and women. They perceive truth; but truth cannot be perceived until it exists; and there can be no truth until there is a mind to perceive it. Truth does not exist apart from mind. Washington and Lincoln were in touch and communication with a mind that knew all knowledge and contained all truth. So of all who manifest wisdom.

Wisdom is obtained by reading the mind of God.

Chapter Three

The Mind of God

There is a Cosmic Intelligence that is in all things and through all things. This is the one real substance. From it all things proceed. It is Intelligent Substance or Mind Stuff. It is God.

Where there is thought there must be a substance which thinks. But thought is not in the brain substance, for brain substance, without life, is quite unintelligent and dead. Thought is the life-principle that animates the brain, in the spirit-substance, which is the real man. The brain does not think, the man thinks and expresses his thought through the brain.

There is a spirit substance that thinks. Just as the spirit substance of man permeates his body, and thinks and knows in the body, so the Original Spirit Substance, God, permeates all nature and thinks and knows in nature. The All-Mind has been in touch with all things from the beginning, and it contains all knowledge. The truths men perceive by inspiration are thoughts held in the mind.

Man is thinking substance, a portion of the Cosmic Substance; but man is limited, while the Cosmic Intelligence from which he sprang, which Jesus calls the Father, is unlimited. All intelligence, power, and force come from the Father. Jesus recognized this and stated it very plainly. Over and over again, he ascribed all his wisdom and power to his unity with the Father, and to his perceiving the thoughts of God. "My father and I are one." This was the foundation of his knowledge and power.

CHAPTER FOUR

Consecration

No one will deny the statement that if you are to be great, the greatness must be a manifestation of something within; nor can you question that this something must be the very greatest and highest that is within. It is not the mind, or the intellect, or the reason. You cannot be great if you go no farther back for principle than to your reasoning power. Reason knows neither principle nor morality. Your reason is like a lawyer in that it will argue for either side. The intellect of a thief will plan robbery or murder as readily as the intellect of a saint will plan a great philanthropy.

Intellect helps us to see the best means and manner of doing the right thing, but intellect never shows us the right thing. Intellect and reason serve the selfish man for his selfish ends as readily as they serve the unselfish man for his unselfish ends. Use intellect and reason without regard to principle, and you may become known as a very able person, but you will never become known as a person whose life shows the power of real greatness.

There is too much training of the intellect and reasoning powers and too little training in obedience to the soul. This is the only thing that can be wrong with your personal attitude—when it fails to be one of obedience to the Principle of Power.

By going back to your own center you can always find the pure idea of right for every relationship. To be great and to have power it is only necessary to conform your life to the pure idea as you find it in the GREAT WITHIN. Every compromise on this point is made at the expense of a loss of power. This you *must* remember.

There are many ideas in your mind that you have outgrown, and which, from force of habit, you still permit to dictate the actions of your life. Cease all this; abandon everything you have outgrown. There are many ignoble customs, social and other, which you still follow, although you know they tend to dwarf and belittle you and keep you acting in a small way. Rise above all this. I do not say that you should absolutely disregard conventionalities, or the commonly accepted standards of right and wrong. You cannot do this; but you can deliver your soul from most of the narrow restrictions which bind the majority of your fellow men.

Do not give your time and strength to the support of obsolete institutions, religious or otherwise; do not be bound by creed in which you do not believe. Be free.

You have perhaps formed some sensual habits of mind or body; abandon them. You still indulge in distrustful fears that things will go wrong, or that people will betray you, or mistreat you; get above all of them. You still act selfishly in many ways and on many occasions; cease to do so. Abandon all these, and in place of them put the best actions you can form a conception of in your mind. If you desire to advance, and you are not doing so, remember that it can be only because your thought is better than your practice. You must do as well as you think.

Let your attitude in business, in politics, in neighborhood affairs, and in your own home be the expression of the best thoughts you can think. Let your manner toward all men and women, great and small, and especially to your own family circle, always be the most kindly, gracious, and courteous you can picture in your imagination.

Say: "I surrender my body to be ruled by my mind; I surrender my mind to be governed by my soul; and I surrender my soul to the guidance of God."

CHAPTER FIVE

Identification

Having recognized God as the advancing presence in nature, society, and your fellow men, and harmonized yourself with all these, and having consecrated yourself to that within you which impels toward the greatest and the highest, the next step is to become aware of and recognize fully the fact that the Principle of Power within you is God Himself. You must consciously identify yourself with the Highest. This is not some false or untrue position to be assumed; it is a fact to be recognized. You are already one with God; you want to become consciously aware of it.

There is one substance, the source of all things, and this substance has within itself the power that creates all things; all power is inherent in it. There cannot be one kind of intelligence in God and another kind of intelligence in man. Man is of one stuff with God, and so all the talents, powers, and possibilities that are in God are in man; not in a few exceptional men but in every man.

The Principle of Power in man is man himself, and man himself is God. But while man is original substance, and has within him all the power and possibilities, his consciousness is limited. He does not know all there is to know, and so he is liable to error and mistake. To save himself from these he must unite his mind to That outside him which does know all; he must become consciously one with God. There is a Mind surrounding him on every side, closer than breathing, nearer than hands and feet, and in this mind is the memory of all that has ever happened, from the greatest convulsions of nature in prehistoric days to the fall of a sparrow in the present time; and all that is in existence now as well. Held in this Mind is the great purpose that is behind all nature, and so it knows what is going to be.

Man is surrounded by a Mind that knows all there is to know, past, present, and to come. Everything that men have said or done or written is present there. Man is of one identical stuff with this Mind; he proceeded from it; and he can so identify himself with it that he may know what it knows.

You must affirm, "There is only one and that one is everywhere. I surrender myself to conscious unity with the highest. Not I, but the Father. I will to be one with the Supreme and to lead the divine life. I am one with infinite consciousness; there is but one mind, and I am that mind. I that speak unto you am he."

CHAPTER SIX

Idealization

A thought held in thinking substance is a real thing; a form, and has actual existence, although it is not visible to you. You internally take the form in which you think of yourself; and you surround yourself with the invisible forms of those things with which you associate in your thoughts.

If you desire a thing, picture it clearly and hold the picture steadily in mind until it becomes a definite thought-form; and if your practices are not such as to separate you from God, the thing you want will come to you in material form. It must do so in obedience to the law by which the universe was created.

Make a thought-form of yourself as strong and hearty and perfectly well; impress this thought-form on creative intelligence, and if your practices are not in violation of the laws by which the physical body is built, your thought-form will become manifest in your flesh. This also is certain; it comes by obedience to law.

Fix upon your ideal of what you wish to make of yourself; consider well and be sure that you make the right choice; that is, the one that will be the most satisfactory to you in a general way. Do not pay too much attention to the advice or suggestions of those around you: do not believe that any one can know, better than yourself, what is right for you. Listen to what others have to say, but always form your own conclusions. DO NOT LET OTHER PEOPLE DECIDE WHAT YOU ARE TO BE. BE WHAT YOU FEEL THAT YOU WANT TO BE.

Do not be misled by a false notion of obligation or duty. You can owe no possible obligation or duty to others that should prevent you from making the most of yourself.

Be true to yourself, and you cannot then be false to any man. When you have fully decided what thing you want to be, form the highest conception of that thing that you are capable of imagining, and make that conception a thought-form. Hold that thought-form as a fact, as the real truth about yourself, and believe in it.

Chapter Seven

Realization

If you were to stop with the close of the last chapter, you would never become great; you would be indeed a mere dreamer of dreams, a castle-builder. Too many do stop there; they do not understand the necessity for present action in realizing the vision and bringing the thought-form into manifestation. Two things are necessary; firstly, the making of the thought-form and secondly, the actual appropriation to yourself of all that goes into, and around, the thought-form.

We have discussed the first, now we will proceed to give directions for the second. When you have made your thought-form, you are already, in your interior, what you want to be; next you must become externally what you want to be. You are already great within, but you are not yet doing the great things without. You cannot begin, on the instant, to do the great things; you cannot be before the world the great actor, or lawyer, or musician, or personality you know yourself to be; no one will entrust great things to you as yet for you have not made yourself known. But you can always begin to do small things in a great way.

Here lies the whole secret. You can begin to be great today in your own home, in your store or office, on the street, everywhere; you can begin to make yourself known as great, and you can do this by doing everything you do in a great way. You must put the whole power of your great soul into every act, however small and commonplace, and so reveal to your family, your friends, and neighbors what you really are. Do not brag or boast of yourself; do not go about telling people what a great personage you are, simply live in a great way. In your domestic circle be so just, so generous, so courteous, and kindly that your family, your wife, husband, children, brothers, and sisters shall know that you are a great and noble soul. In all your relations with men be great, just, generous, courteous, and kindly. The great are never otherwise. This is your attitude.

Next, and most important, you must have absolute faith in your own perceptions of truth. Never act in haste or hurry; be deliberate in everything; wait until you feel that you know the true way. And when you do feel that you know the true way, be guided by your own faith though the entire world shall disagree with you. If you do not believe what God tells you in little things, you will never draw upon his wisdom and knowledge in larger things. When you feel deeply that a certain act is the right act, do it and have perfect faith that the consequences will be good.

Rely upon your perception of truth in all the facts and circumstances of life. If you deeply feel that a certain man will be in a certain place on a certain day, go there with perfect faith to meet him; he will be there, no matter how unlikely it may seem. If you feel sure that certain people are making certain combinations, or doing certain things, act in the faith that they are doing those things. If you feel sure of the truth of any circumstance or happening, near or distant, past, present, or to come, trust in your perception. You may make occasional mistakes at first because of your imperfect understanding of the within; but you will soon be guided almost invariably right. Soon your family and friends will begin to defer, more and more, to your judgment and to be guided by you. Soon your neighbors and townsmen will be coming to you for counsel and advice; soon you will be recognized as one who is great in small things, and you will be called upon more and more to take charge of larger things.

Chapter Eight

Hurry and Habit

No doubt you have many problems, domestic, social, physical, and financial, which seem to you to be pressing for instant solution. You have debts that must be paid, or other obligations that must be met; you are unhappily or inharmoniously placed, and feel that something must be done at once. Do not get into a hurry and act from superficial impulses. You can trust God for the solution of all your personal riddles. There is no hurry. There is only God, and all is well with the world.

There is an invincible power in you, and the same power is in the things you want. It is bringing them to you and bringing you to them. This is a thought that you must grasp, and hold continuously—that the same intelligence that is in you is in the things you desire. They are impelled toward you as strongly and decidedly as your desire impels you toward them. The tendency, therefore, of a steadily held thought must be to bring the things you desire to you and to group them around you. So long as you hold your thought and your faith right, all must go well. *Nothing can be wrong but your own personal attitude, and that will not be wrong if you trust and are not afraid.* Hurry is a manifestation of fear; he who fears not has plenty of time. If you act with perfect faith in your own perceptions of truth, you will never be too late or too early

Next, as to habit, it is probable that your greatest difficulty will be to overcome your old habitual ways of thought, and to form new habits. The world is ruled by habit. Kings, tyrants, masters, and plutocrats hold their positions solely because the people have come to habitually accept them. Things are as they are only because people have formed the habit of accepting them as they are. When the people change their habitual thought about governmental, social, and industrial institutions, they will change the institutions. Habit rules us all.

You have formed, perhaps, the habit of thinking of yourself as a common person, as one of a limited ability, or as being more or less of a failure. Whatever you habitually think yourself to be, that you are. You must form, now, a greater and better habit; you must form a conception of yourself as a being of limitless power, and habitually think that you are that being. It is the habitual, not the periodical thought that decides your destiny. It will avail you nothing to sit apart for a few moments several times a day to affirm that you are great, if during all the balance of the day, while you are about your regular vocation, you think of yourself as not great. No amount of praying or affirmation will make you great if you still habitually regard yourself as being small. The use of prayer and affirmation is to change your habit of thought.

Any act, mental or physical, often repeated, becomes a habit. The purpose of mental exercises is to repeat certain thoughts over and over until the thinking of those thoughts becomes constant and habitual. The thoughts we continually repeat become convictions. What you must do is to repeat the new thought of yourself until it is the only way in which you think of yourself. Habitual thought, and not environment or circumstance, has made you what you are. Every person has some central idea or thought-form of himself, and by this idea he classifies and arranges all his facts and external relationships. You are classifying your facts either according to the idea that you are a great and strong personality, or according to the idea that you are limited, common, or weak. If the latter is the case you must change your central idea. Get a new mental picture of yourself. Do not try to become great by repeating mere strings of words or superficial formulas; but repeat over and over the THOUGHT of your own power and ability until you classify external facts, and decide your place everywhere by this idea.

Chapter Nine

Thought

Greatness is only attained by the constant thinking of great thoughts. No man can become great in outward personality until he is great internally; and no man can be great internally until he THINKS. No amount of education, reading, or study can make you great without thought; but thought can make you great with very little study. There are altogether too many people who are trying to make something of themselves by reading books without thinking; all such will fail. You are not mentally developed by what you read, but by what you think about what you read.

Thinking is the hardest and most exhausting of all labor; and hence many people shrink from it. God has so formed us that we are continuously impelled to thought; we must either think or engage in some activity to escape thought. The headlong, continuous chase for pleasure in which most people spend all their leisure time is only an effort to escape thought. If they are alone, or if they have nothing amusing to take their attention, as a novel to read or a show to see, they must think; and to escape from thinking they resort to novels, shows, and all the endless devices of the purveyors of amusement. Most people spend the greater part of their leisure time running away from thought, hence they are where they are.

Read about great things and think about great questions and issues. Thinking, not mere knowledge or information, makes personality. Thinking is growth; you cannot think without growing. Every thought engenders another thought. There can be no real greatness without original thought.

Action is the second form of thought, and personality is the materialization of thought. Environment is the result of thought; things group themselves or arrange themselves around you according to your thought. There is, as Emerson says, some central idea or conception of yourself by which all the facts of your life are arranged and classified. Change this central idea and you change the arrangement or classification of all the facts and circumstances of your life.

CHAPTER TEN

Action at Home

D o not merely think that you are going to become great; think *that you are great now.* Do
not think that you will begin to act in a great
way at some future time; begin now.

If you are not in an environment where there is scope
for your best powers and talents you can move in due
time; but meanwhile you can be great where you are.

Never mind how the people around you, including
those of your own household, may treat you. That has
nothing at all to do with your being great; that is, it
cannot hinder you from being great. People may ne-
glect you and be unthankful and unkind in their attitude toward you; does that prevent you from being
great in your manner and attitude toward them? "Your
Father," said Jesus, "is kind to the unthankful and the
evil." Would God be great if he should go away and sulk
because people were unthankful and did not appreciate

him? Treat the unthankful and the evil in a great and perfectly kind way, just as God does.

Then assume the same mental attitude with your neighbors, friends, and those you meet in business, you will soon find that people are beginning to depend on you. Your advice will be sought, and a constantly increasing number of people will look to you for strength and inspiration, and rely upon your judgment. Here, as in the home, you must avoid meddling with other people's affairs. Help all who come to you, but do not go about officiously endeavoring to set other people right. Mind your own business. It is no part of your mission in life to correct people's morals, habits, or practices. Lead a great life, doing all things with a great spirit and in a great way; give to him that asketh of you as freely as you have received, but do not force your help or your opinions upon any man.

Form your mental vision of yourself with care. Make the thought-form of yourself as you wish to be, and hold this with the faith that it is being realized, and with the purpose to realize it completely. Do every common act as a god should do it; speak every word as a god should speak it; meet men and women of both low and high estate as a god meets other divine beings. Begin thus and continue thus, and your unfoldment in ability and power will be great and rapid.

CHAPTER ELEVEN

Jesus's Idea of Greatness

I n the twenty-third chapter of Matthew, Jesus makes a very plain distinction between true and false greatness; and also points out the one great danger to all who wish to become great. Speaking to the multitude and to his disciples he bids them beware of adopting the principle of the Pharisees. He points out that while the Pharisees are just and righteous men, honorable judges, true lawgivers and upright in their dealings with men, they "love the uppermost seats at feasts and greetings in the marketplace, and to be called Master, Master"; and in comparison with this principle, he says: "He that will be great among you let him serve."

The average person's idea of a great man, rather than of one who serves, is of one who succeeds in getting himself served. He gets himself in a position to command men; to exercise power over them, making them obey his will. The exercise of dominion over other people, to most persons, is a great thing. Nothing seems to be sweeter to the selfish soul than this. You will always find every selfish and undeveloped person trying to domineer over others, to exercise control over other men. Savage men were no sooner placed upon the earth than they began to enslave one another. For ages the struggle in war, diplomacy, politics, and government has been aimed at the securing of control over other men. Kings and princes have drenched the soil of the earth in blood and tears in the effort to extend their dominions and their power to rule more people. The struggle of the business world today is the same as that on the battlefields of Europe a century ago so far as the ruling principle is concerned.

I want you to contrast these two ideas of greatness sharply in your minds. "He that will be great among you let him serve." I speak not of servility, but service. Lincoln was a great man because he knew how to be a great servant. Napoleon, able, cold, selfish, seeking the high places, was a brilliant man. Lincoln was great; Napoleon was not.

The very moment you begin to advance and are recognized as one who is doing things in a great way you will find yourself in danger. The temptation to patronize, advise, or take upon yourself the direction of other people's affairs is sometimes almost irresistible. Avoid, however, the opposite danger of falling into servility, or of completely throwing yourself away in the service of others.

Thousands of people imitating Jesus, as they suppose, have belittled themselves and given up all else to go about doing good; practicing an altruism that is really as morbid and as far from great as the rankest selfishness. The finer instincts that respond to the cry of trouble or distress are not by any means all of you; they are not necessarily the best part of you. There are other things you must do besides helping the unfortunate, although it is true that a large part of the life and activities of every great person must be given to helping other people. As you begin to advance they will come to you. Do not turn them away. But do not make the fatal error of supposing that the life of complete self-abnegation is the way of greatness.

CHAPTER TWELVE

Serving God

I have brought you thus far with a view to finally settling the question of duty. This is one that puzzles and perplexes very many people who are earnest and sincere. When they start to make something of themselves and to practice the science of being great, they find themselves necessarily compelled to rearrange many of their relationships. There are friends who perhaps must be alienated, there are relatives who misunderstand and who feel that they are in some way being slighted; the really great man is often considered selfish by a large circle of people who are connected with him and who feel that he might bestow upon them more benefits than he does. The question at the outset is: Is it my duty to make the most of myself regardless of everything else?

The answer lies in service to God. The only service you can render God is to give expression to what he is trying to give the world, through you. The only service you can render God is to make the very most of yourself in order that God may live in you to the utmost of your possibilities. The Spirit of God is over, about, around, and in all of us, seeking to do great things with us, so soon as we will train our hands and feet, our minds, brains, and bodies to do His service.

Your first duty to God, to yourself, and to the world is to make yourself as great a personality, in every way, as you possibly can. And that, it seems to me, disposes of the question of duty.

The world needs demonstration more than it needs teaching. For this mass of people, our duty is to become as great in personality as possible in order that they may see and desire to do likewise. It is our duty to make ourselves great for their sakes; so that we may help prepare the world that the next generation shall have better conditions for thought.

One last point. I frequently hear from people who wish to make something of themselves and to move out into the world, but who are hampered by home ties, having others more or less dependent upon them, whom they fear would suffer if left alone. In general I advise such people to move out fearlessly, and to make the most of themselves. If there is a loss at home it will be only temporary and apparent, for in a little while, if you follow the leading of Spirit, you will be able to take better care of your dependents than you have ever done before.

About the Authors

A progressive social reformer and New Thought pioneer, WALLACE D. WATTLES was born in 1860 in the United States. He popularized creative-thought principles in his groundbreaking classics *The Science of Getting Rich, The Science of Being Great,* and *The Science of Being Well.* A great influence on future generations of success writers, he died in 1911.

MITCH HOROWITZ, who abridged and introduced this volume, is the PEN Award-winning author of books including *Occult America* and *The Miracle Club: How Thoughts Become Reality. The Washington Post* says Mitch "treats esoteric ideas and movements with an even-handed intellectual studiousness that is too often lost in today's raised-voice discussions." Follow him @MitchHorowitz.